STAIND 14 SHADES OF GREY

Special thanks to Mike Mushok for his assistance.
Thanks also to Gayle Boulware and Marie D'Antonio of The Firm.

Transcribed by Hemme Luttjeboer

Project Manager: Aaron Stang
Music Editor: Colgan Bryan
Book Art Layout: JP Creative Group
Album Artwork: © 2003 Flip Records & Elektra Entertainment Group Inc.
Photography: Anthony Mandler

+ PRICE TO PLAY We fail to see How destructive we can be Taking without giving back 'Til the damage can be seen Can you see? Can you see? / Chorus - The more you take, the more you blame But everything still feels the same The more you hurt, the more you strain The price you pay to play the game And all you seek, and all you gain And all you step on with no shame There are no rules, no one to blame The price you pay to play the game / Apathy, the chosen way to be Blindly look the other way While you waste away with me Can you see? Can you see? / Chorus / What you pay to play the game (x4) / Chorus / What you pay to play the game (x4)

+ HOW ABOUT YOU If someone else showed you the way Would you take the wheel and steer? It hurts me that you're not ashamed Of what you're doing here If they jumped off a bridge Would you meet them on the ground? Or would you try and claim That it never made a sound? / Chorus - Everyone plays the hand they're dealt And learns to walk through life themselves Not everything in life is handed on a plate When people think your words are true It doesn't matter what you do I sold my soul to get here How 'bout you? / So you choose to force your hand What a strange way to make friends And you always change the rules So the drama never ends And you blindly go through life Judging only by its worth Just try not to forget That the meek inherit earth / Chorus / So please don't take offense This is just a point of view 'Cause I'm the only one who Will say these things to you / Chorus

+ SO FAR AWAY This is my life It's not what it was before All these feelings I've shared And these are my dreams That I'd never lived before Somebody shake me 'cause I I must be sleeping / Chorus - Now that we're here, it's so far away All the struggle we thought was in vain All the mistakes, one life contained They all finally start to go away Now that we're here, it's so far away And I feel like I can face the day I can forgive, and I'm not ashamed To be the person that I am today / These are my words That I've never said before I think I'm doing okay And this is the smile That I've never shown before Somebody shake me 'cause I I must be sleeping / Chorus / I'm so afraid of waking Please don't shake me Afraid of waking Please don't shake me / Chorus

+ YESTERDAY You don't know what you've put me through It's okay, I've forgiven you But in some way, hope it fucks with you Hope it fucks with you / Pre-Chorus - That I'm okay and I've made it through But who's to say what you're going through I'll say no names, though I've wanted to Isn't it strange how it seems like... / Chorus - Yesterday, a boy and already afraid Locked deep inside, my place to hide To hide from how you made me feel And I wonder how's your brother Did he end up fucked up like me? Lost in himself, crying for help It's safe to say / I learned to live without a pride Just a shell, with me stuck inside A prison, not a place to hide Not a place to hide / Pre-Chorus / Chorus / Chorus (altered) - Yesterday, a boy and already afraid Locked deep inside, my place to hide To hide from how you made me feel And I wonder how's your brother Did he finally pull through like me? Finding himself, not needing help I'd like to say

+ FRAY I know that it never goes away All I feel, everything I'm not today So I try and I try to make everything right I don't feel like I'm doing it, it affects me / Chorus - You wouldn't listen even if I told you Who the fuck am I to say? You're too busy with the lies they sold you Another cure to fix your day Open wide for all the shit they feed you While the TV defecates And blindly walk wherever they will lead you While the edges slowly fray / I know that everything can change What I need is to open up again So never again will I look back in vain 'Cause today's not the past, I don't need to relive it / Chorus / Are you satisfied? I've given all I can And are you pacified Or do you want more from me? / Chorus / I've learned that this life's not just a game Just a line between the pleasures and the pain / Chorus

+ ZOE JANE Well I want you to notice To notice when I'm not around And I know that your eyes see straight through me And speak to me without a sound / Chorus - I want to hold you Protect you from all of the things I've already endured And I want to show you To show you all of the things that this life has in store for you I'll always love you The way that a father should love his daughter / When I walked out this morning I cried as I walked to the door I cried about how long I'd be away for I cried about leaving you all alone / Chorus / Sweet Zoe Jane (x2) / So I wanted to say this 'Cause I wouldn't know where to begin To explain to you what I have been through To explain where your daddy has been / Chorus / Sweet Zoe Jane (x2)

+ **FILL ME UP** I just had to let you know 'Cause I don't always let it show You give me needed room to grow And I just had to tell you so / Chorus - You fill me up, you're in my veins A look could take my breath away And all these things, you give away Sometimes I take for granted / It's just like poetry inside To hear you breathing by my side Like I'm in heaven and I've died So glad you're with me for this ride / Chorus / I see your face to start my day Makes all my bad dreams go away And all the stupid games we play Wouldn't have it any other way / Chorus (x2)

+ **LAYNE** I heard today that you were gone I had to stop and sing along The song they played to say goodbye A song that gave, gave me back life / Chorus - You'll never fade The words you gave My life you saved Your name was Layne / And on that day a child was born To someone who you helped along And helped see through his darkest times Because of you, this child she is mine / Chorus / Bridge / The words you said, you made me feel like they were all for me The words you said, they will always be a part of me The words you said, you made me feel like I was not alone The words you said, you gave me all the strength to carry on / Chorus (altered) - So to me you'll never fade Your life you gave My life you saved Your name was Layne

+ **FALLING DOWN** What's happened to you? It's obvious you've changed Something deep inside you is probably to blame Must be lonely up there with your head up in the clouds Even though you got there what does your conscience tell you now? / Chorus - It's never the same on the way down How does it feel when your feet finally hit the ground? When all of your bridges aren't around And the sandcastles you built are falling down / You had us all sitting right there in your hand But you had to fall because that's how this life is Got your fingers burned by burning candles at both ends Now the table's turned and now your demons are your friends / Chorus / Bridge / So now I question what you're gonna do Now that everything's gone up with you You believe the shit you say is true But everybody's on to you Life remembers everything you do Your karma has caught up with you / Chorus

+ **REALITY** The lights are on but you're not home You've drifted off somewhere alone Somewhere that's safe, no questions here A quiet place where you hide from your fears / Chorus - Sometimes when you're out of rope The way to climb back up's unclear The walls you build around yourself I guess they also keep you here Are you afraid of what they think? Whoever "they" happen to be Or are you hiding from the scars of your own reality? / So you sedate and drown in vain You've got a pill for every day A suit and tie to mask the truth Its ugly head is starting to show through / Chorus / Bridge / The monster you're feeding, your lack of perception The things you will do to fulfill addictions The light at the end of your tunnel is closing What is it that you're so afraid of exposing You'd give it all up for what's there for the taking Whatever it takes to keep your hands from shaking The same things you're thinking might make you feel better The same things that probably got you here / Chorus / Bridge

+ **TONIGHT** Just try to understand this isn't what I planned This ride's out of my hands So now I'm forced to be something I cannot be If only I could make you see / Chorus - Tonight I'm alive I've watched you all grow up and so have I Inside this isn't really what I had in mind / I no longer relate to this world of hate That's forced upon my plate I tend to disagree, I hope it's not just me, alone If only I could make you see / Chorus (x3)

+ **COULD IT BE** Well I don't know what to say Because there's truth to what you say I know it kills you I'm this way There's something different every day / Chorus - Could it be that I never had the chance to grow inside? Could it be that my habit is to find a place to hide? Could it be that sometimes I say things just to disagree? Could it be that I'm only being me? / Not easy living in my mind A little peace is hard to find My every thought is undermined By all the history inside / Chorus / Bridge / I know I hear the words you said Over and over again I just can't get them through my head There's just too many voices Must be like living with the dead Waiting for me to begin To do the things that I have said And for this I'm / sorry So there's some truth to what you say / Chorus

+ **BLOW AWAY** Live in my head for just one day I see myself and look away The road is showing now on my face Soon I'll disappear, I'll disappear without a fucking trace / Chorus - Faces that I've seen turn old and grey I've lost too many friends along the way Memories I never thought would fade They fade and blow away / I wish that I could disappear Unzip my skin and leave it here So I could be no one again And never let nobody, I'd let nobody, I'd let nobody in / Chorus / So now the walls are closing in Because in life you sink or swim Sometimes these shoes don't feel right in my head Feel like a book that can't be, a book that can't be, a book that can't be read / Chorus

+ **INTRO** Thank you to the people in my life For putting up with me And thank you for the time you sacrificed All on account of me / Chorus - For all the times I didn't say The times I didn't say For all the times I didn't say The times I didn't say / Fuck you to the jaded and the fake Like to see what you would do Fuck you and the judgments that you make We're not all perfect just like you, like you, like you / Chorus / All the times I didn't say (x2) / Thank you to the people in my life for putting up with me

PRICE TO PLAY

All gtrs. tuned to:
⑥ = G♭ ③ = D♭
⑤ = D♭ ② = G♭
④ = A♭ ① = B♭

Music by MICHAEL MUSHOK,
AARON LEWIS, JOHN APRIL
and JONATHAN WYSOCKI
Lyrics by AARON LEWIS

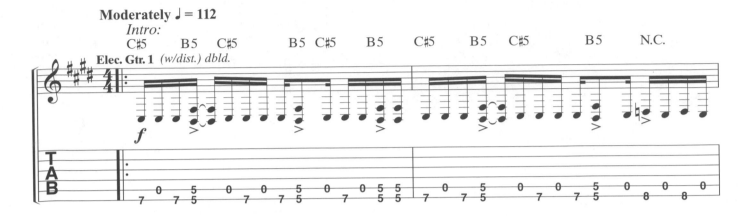

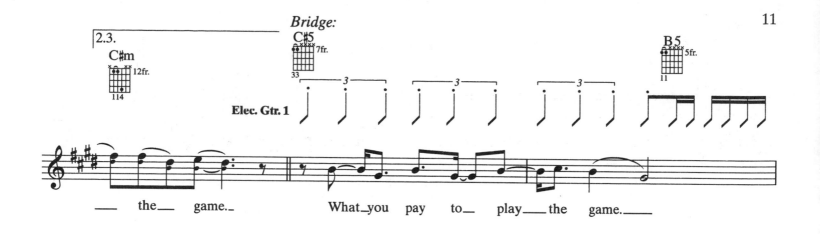

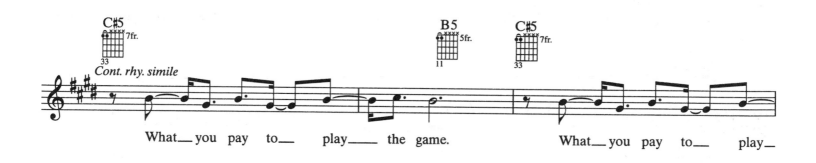

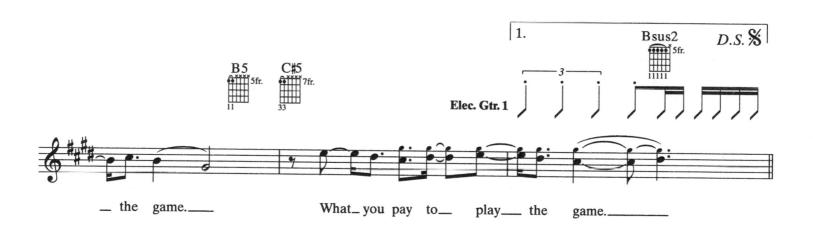

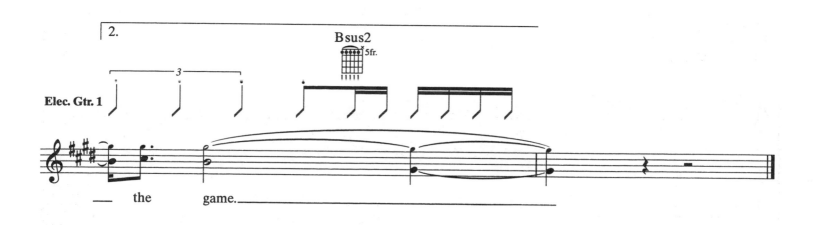

HOW ABOUT YOU

Elec. Gtrs. 1 & 2 tuned:

⑥ = A♭   ③ = D♭
⑤ = E♭   ② = E♭
④ = A♭   ① = A♭

Acous. Gtr. 1 & Elec. Gtr. 3 tuned down 1/2 step:

⑥ = E♭   ③ = G♭
⑤ = A♭   ② = B♭
④ = D♭   ① = E♭

Music by MICHAEL MUSHOK,
AARON LEWIS, JOHN APRIL
and JONATHAN WYSOCKI
Lyrics by AARON LEWIS

13

How About You - 6 - 2

PGM0313

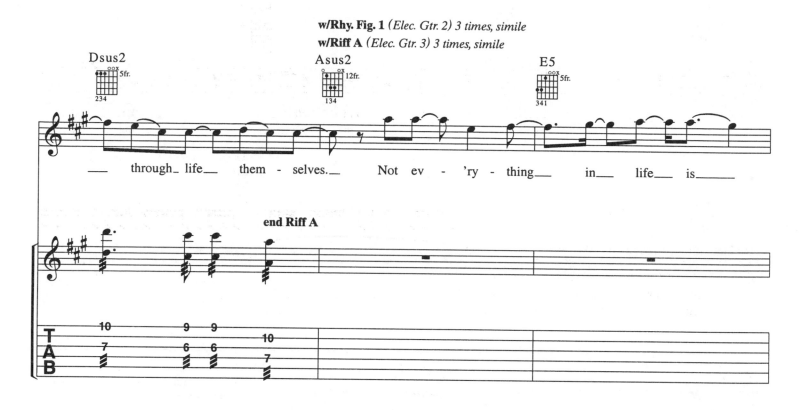

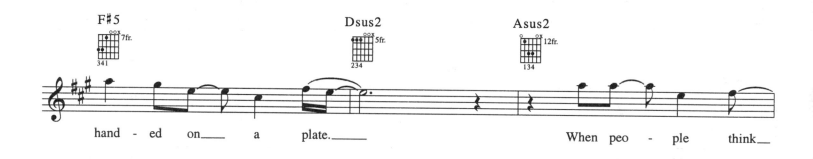

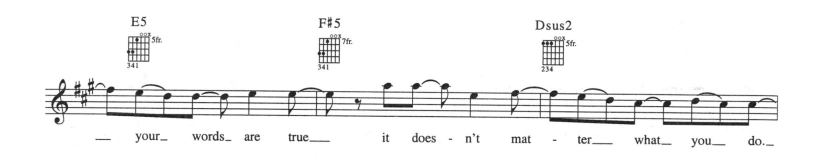

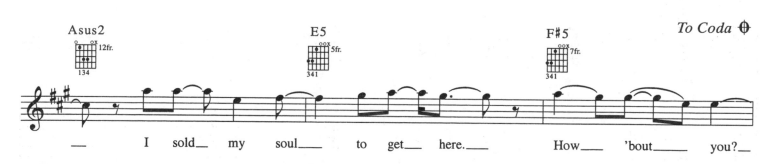

16

17

SO FAR AWAY

Elec. Gtrs. 1 & 2 tuned:

⑥ = A♭   ③ = D♭
⑤ = E♭   ② = E♭
④ = A♭   ① = A♭

Acous. Gtr. 1 & Elec. Gtr. 3 tuned down 1/2 step:

⑥ = E♭   ③ = G♭
⑤ = A♭   ② = B♭
④ = D♭   ① = E♭

Music by MICHAEL MUSHOK,
AARON LEWIS, JOHN APRIL
and JONATHAN WYSOCKI
Lyrics by AARON LEWIS

Slowly ♩. = 45 (♪ = 135)
Intro:

20

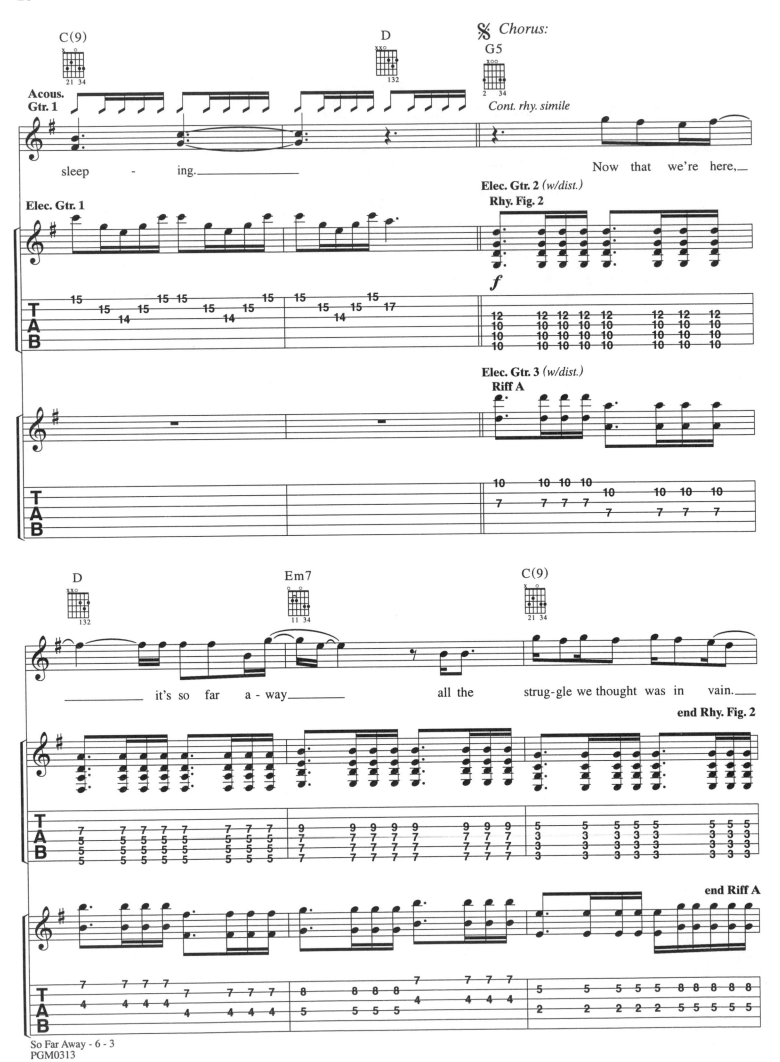

22

So Far Away - 6 - 5
PGM0313

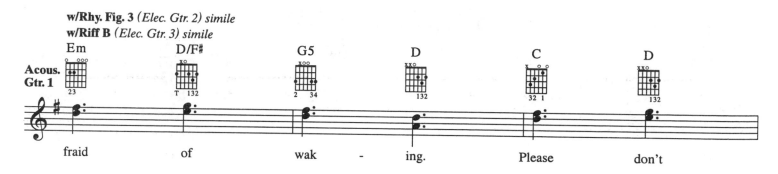

w/Rhy. Fig. 3 *(Elec. Gtr. 2) simile*
w/Riff B *(Elec. Gtr. 3) simile*

fraid   of   wak - ing.   Please   don't

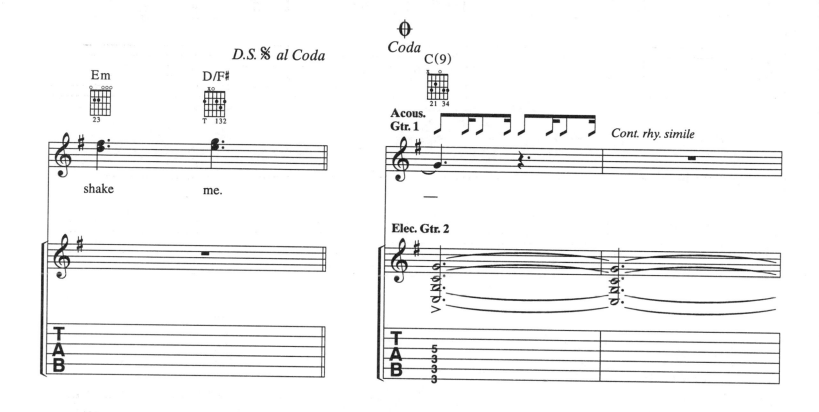

D.S. % al Coda   *Coda*

shake   me.

Acous. Gtr. 1

Cont. rhy. simile

Elec. Gtr. 2

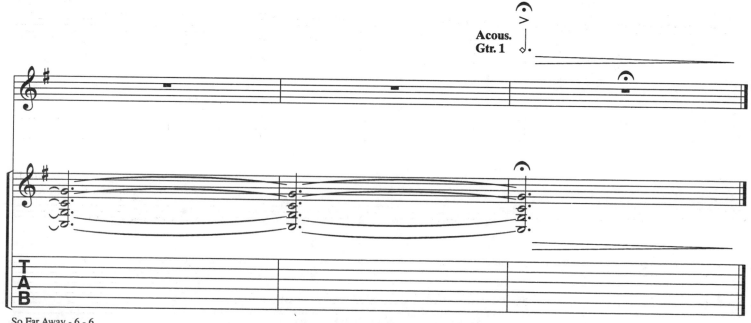

Acous. Gtr. 1

YESTERDAY

Music by MICHAEL MUSHOK,
AARON LEWIS, JOHN APRIL
and JONATHAN WYSOCKI
Lyrics by AARON LEWIS

All gtrs. tuned:

⑥ = A♭   ③ = D♭
⑤ = E♭   ② = E♭
④ = B♭   ① = A♭

Moderately ♩ = 118
Intro:

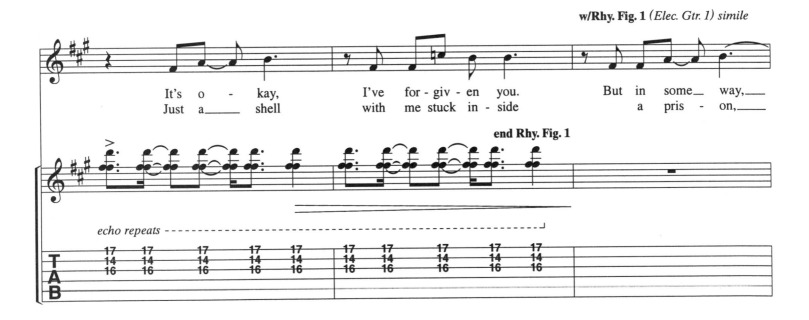

Pre-chorus:

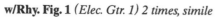

w/Rhy. Fig. 1 *(Elec. Gtr. 1) 2 times, simile*

That I'm____ o - kay____ and I've made it through.___

___ But who's___ to say___ what you're go - ing through?___

___ I'll say___ no names,___ though I've want - ed to.___

___ Is - n't___ it strange___ how it seems like

Yesterday - 5 - 2
PGM0313

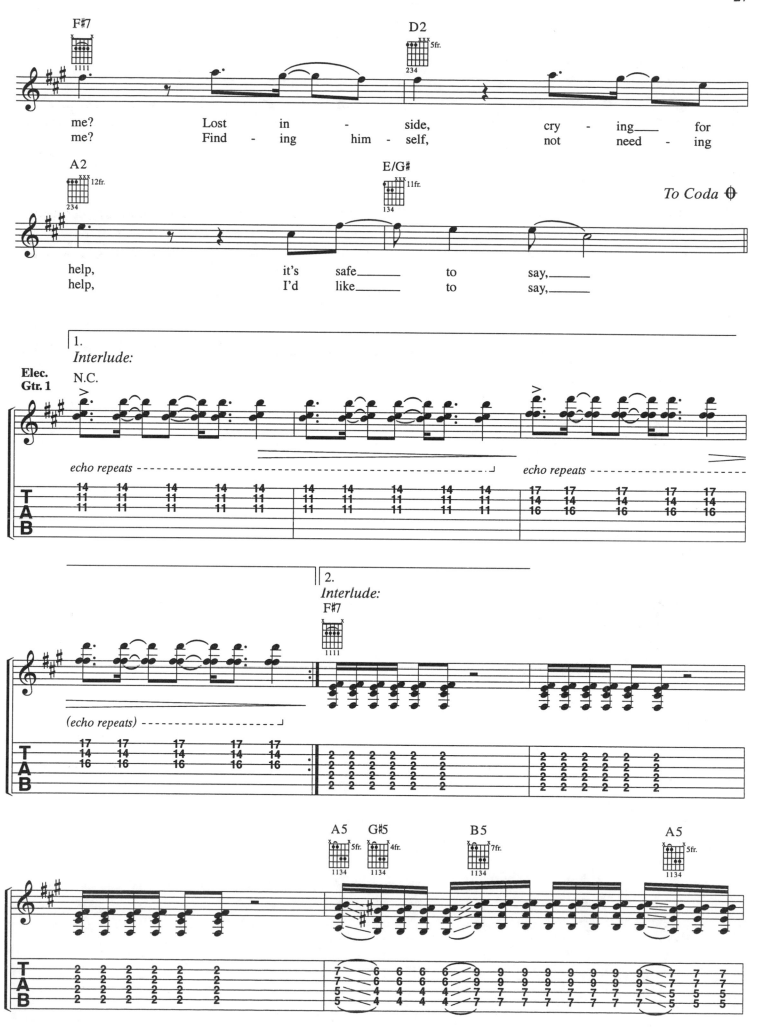

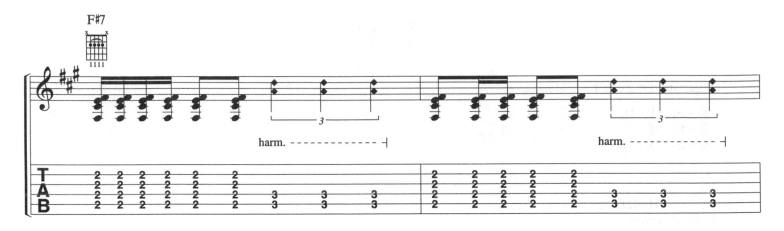

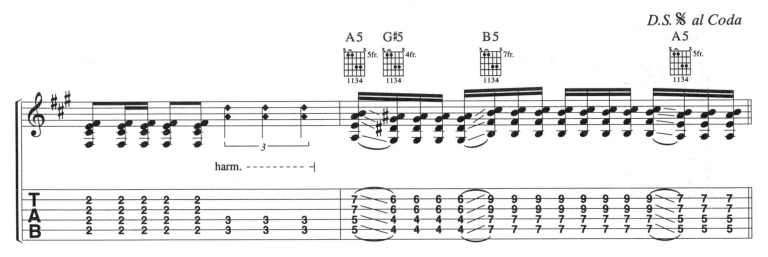

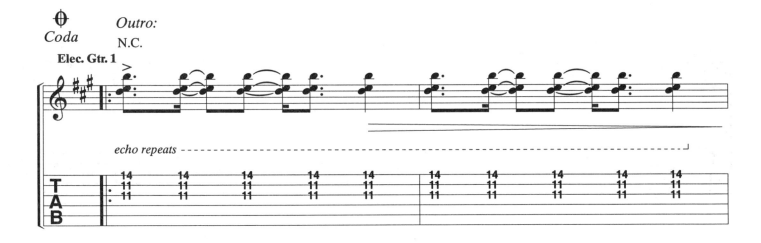

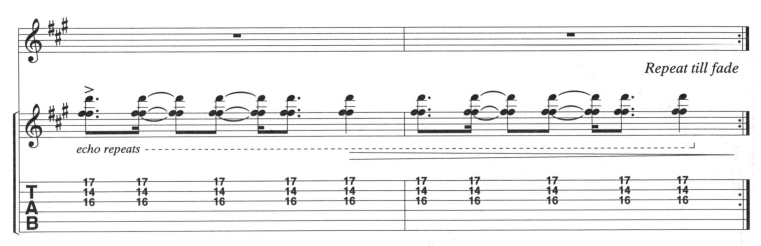

FRAY

Elec. Gtrs. 1 & 2 tuned:

⑥ = A♭ ③ = D♭
⑤ = E♭ ② = F
④ = B♭ ① = B♭

Elec. Gtr. 3 tuned down 1/2 step:

⑥ = E♭ ③ = G♭
⑤ = A♭ ② = B♭
④ = D♭ ① = E♭

Music by MICHAEL MUSHOK,
AARON LEWIS, JOHN APRIL
and JONATHAN WYSOCKI
Lyrics by AARON LEWIS

Moderately slow ♩ = 74
Intro:

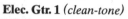

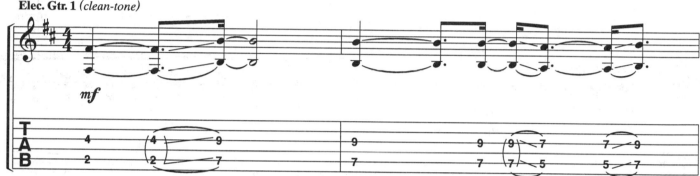

Fray - 7 - 1
PGM0313

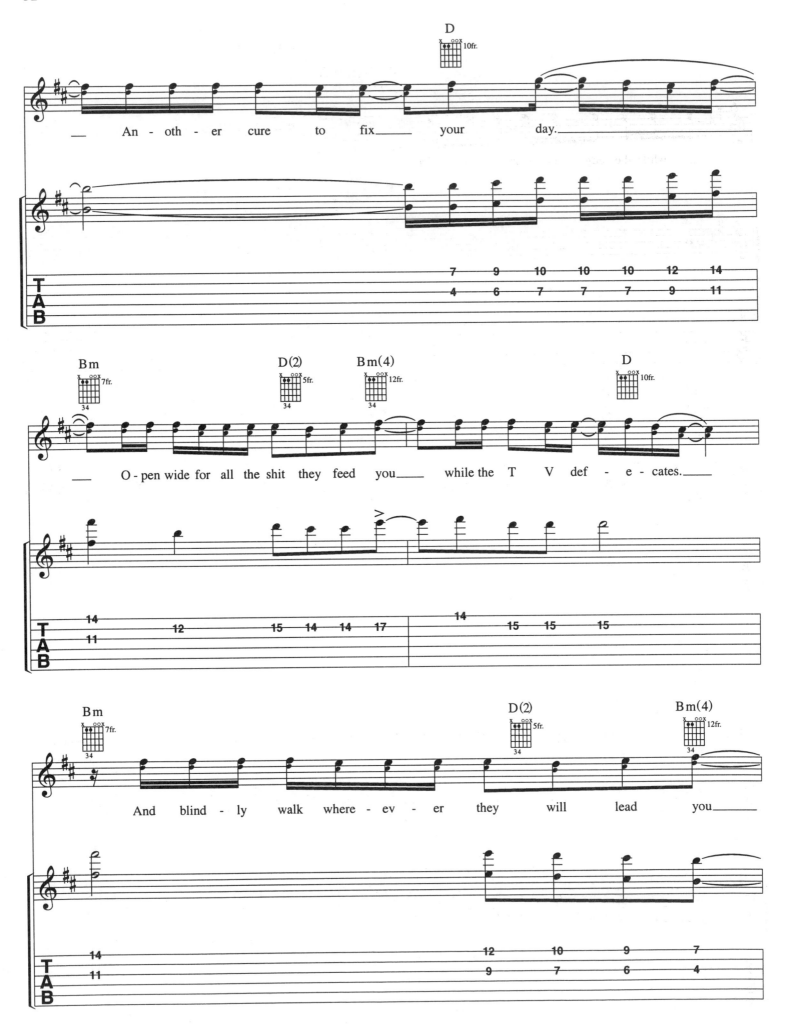

while the edg - es slow - ly fray.

Are you sat - is - fied?

ZOE JANE

Music by MICHAEL MUSHOK,
AARON LEWIS, JOHN APRIL
and JONATHAN WYSOCKI
Lyrics by AARON LEWIS

Elec. Gtrs. tuned:

⑥ = A♭   ③ = D♭
⑤ = D♭   ② = E♭
④ = A♭   ① = A♭

Acous. Gtr. 1 tuned down 1/2 step:

⑥ = E♭   ③ = G♭
⑤ = A♭   ② = B♭
④ = D♭   ① = E♭

Moderately ♩ = 114

Intro:

*Music sounds a half step lower than written.

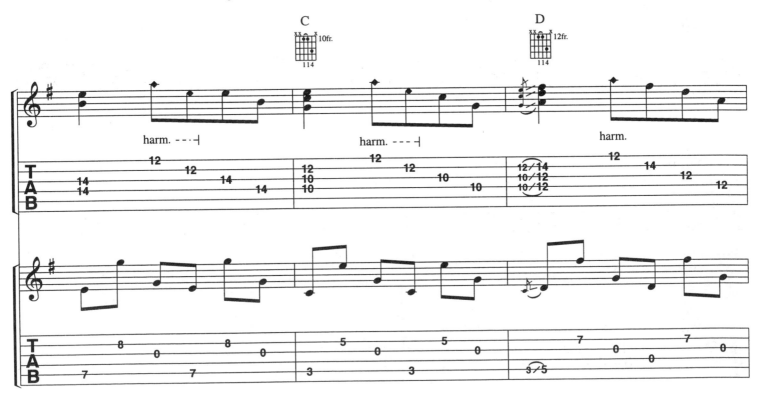

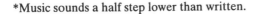

Zoe Jane - 4 - 1
PGM0313

Verse 3:
So I wanted to say this
'Cause I wouldn't know where to begin
To explain to you what I've been through.
To explain where your daddy has been.
(To Chorus:)

FILL ME UP

Elec. Gtrs. 1 & 2 tuned:

⑥ = A♭ ③ = D♭
⑤ = E♭ ② = G♭
④ = B♭ ① = B♭

Elec. Gtrs. 3 & 4 tuned down 1/2 step:

⑥ = E♭ ③ = G♭
⑤ = A♭ ② = B♭
④ = D♭ ① = E♭

Music by MICHAEL MUSHOK,
AARON LEWIS, JOHN APRIL
and JONATHAN WYSOCKI
Lyrics by AARON LEWIS

Moderately ♩ = 104

Intro:

D5 E5 D5 C5 D5 E5 D

Elec. Gtr. 1 *(w/dist.)* **dbld. on repeat**

f

*Music sounds a half step lower than written.

D5 E5 D5 C5 D5 E5 D

1.

2.

% *Verse:*

D5 E5 D Em

1. I_____ just
2. It's just like
3. *See additional lyrics*

Rhy. Fig. 1
Elec. Gtr. 2 *(clean-tone)*

Fill Me Up - 7 - 1
PGM0313

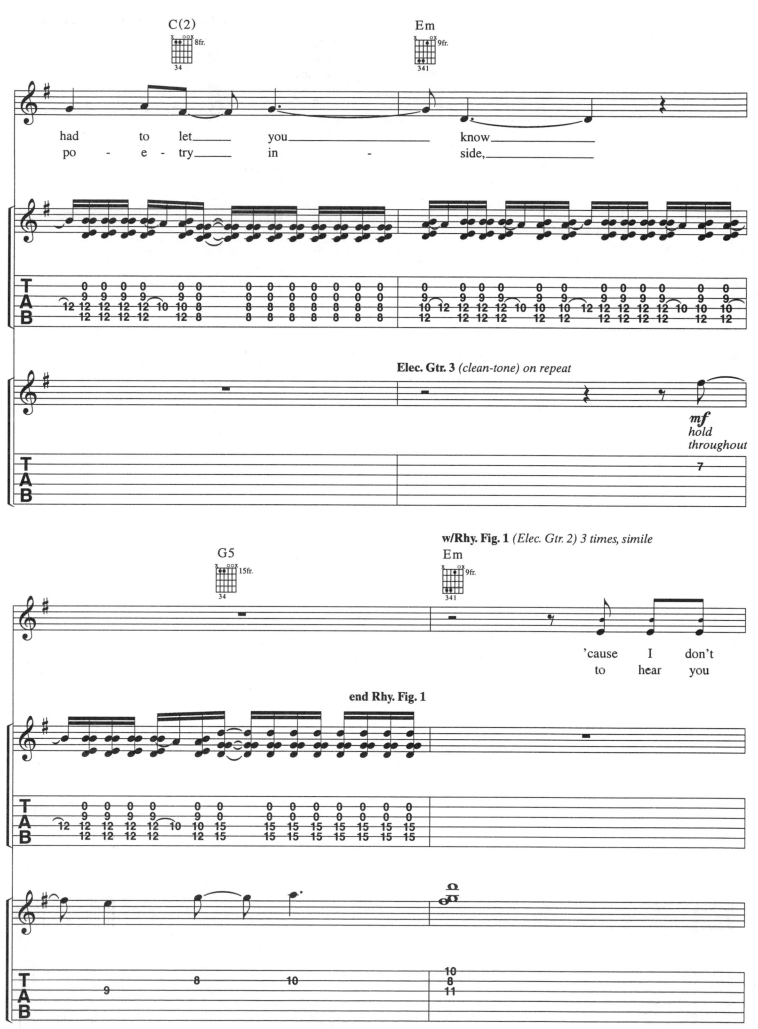

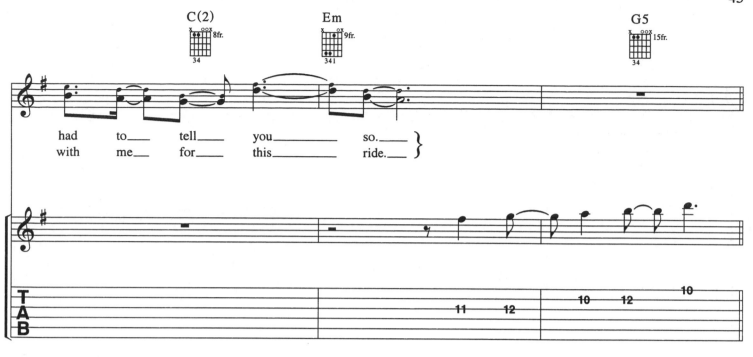

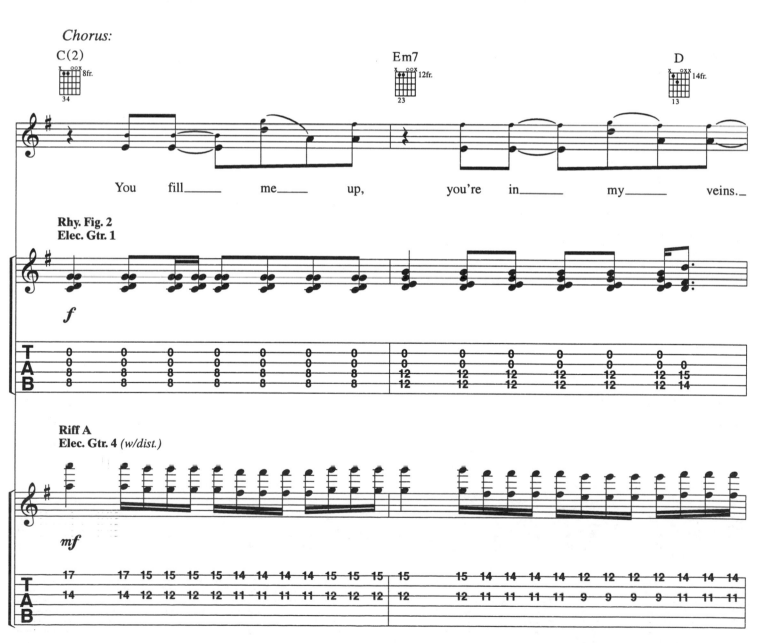

PGM0313

Fill Me Up - 7 - 5
PGM0313

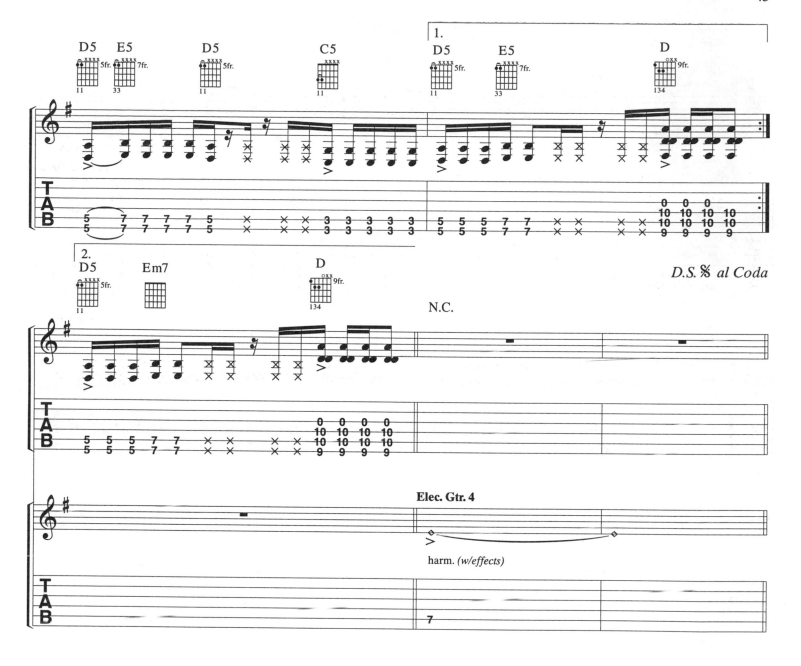

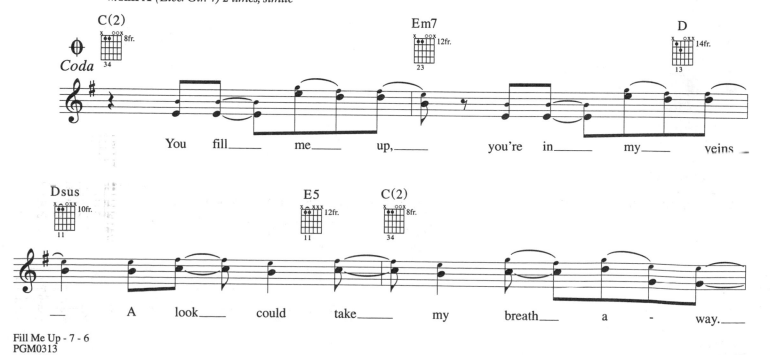

You fill____ me____ up,____ you're in____ my____ veins

____ A look____ could take____ my breath____ a - way.____

Verse 3:
I see your face to start my day.
Makes all my bad dreams go away.
And all the stupid games we play
Wouldn't have it any other way.
(To Chorus:)

LAYNE

Elec. Gtrs. 1 & 2 tuned:
⑥ = A♭   ③ = D♭
⑤ = D♭   ② = E♭
④ = A♭   ① = A♭

Elec. Gtr. 3 tuned down 1 1/2 steps:
⑥ = E♭   ③ = G♭
⑤ = A♭   ② = B♭
④ = D♭   ① = E♭

Music by MICHAEL MUSHOK,
AARON LEWIS, JOHN APRIL
and JONATHAN WYSOCKI
Lyrics by AARON LEWIS

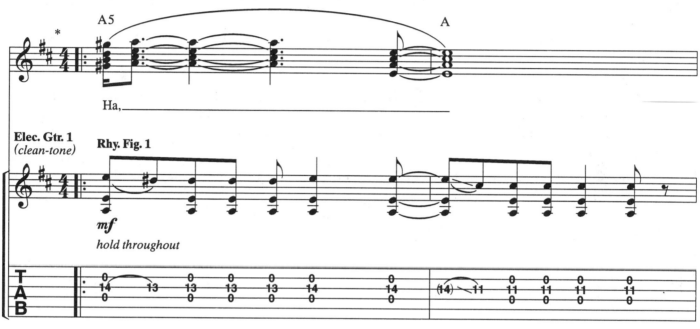

*Music sounds a half step lower than written.

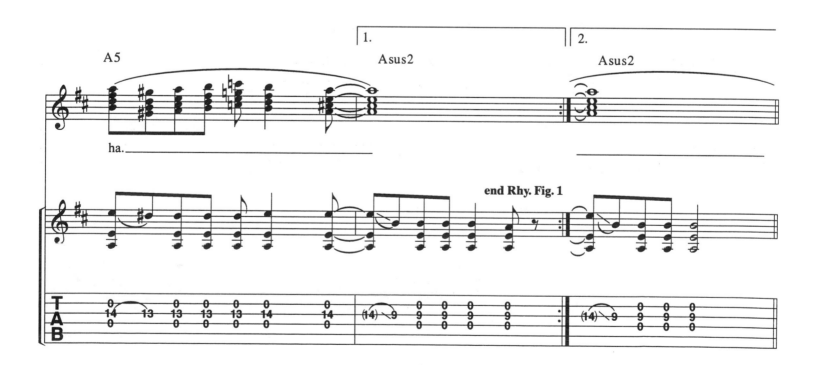

Layne - 6 - 1
PGM0313

50

51

Layne - 6 - 5
PGM0313

FALLING DOWN

All gtrs. tuned:
⑥ = Ab   ③ = Db
⑤ = Eb   ② = Gb
④ = Bb   ① = Bb

Music by MICHAEL MUSHOK,
AARON LEWIS, JOHN APRIL
and JONATHAN WYSOCKI
Lyrics by AARON LEWIS

Moderately fast ♩ = 134

Intro:
Half-time feel

Gsus2

Rhy. Fig. 1

Elec. Gtr. 1 *(clean-tone) dbld. by Elec. Gtr. 2 (w/dist.) on repeat*

*Music sounds a half step lower than written.

Bsus2

end Rhy. Fig. 1

hold --------------------------------

Gsus2

Bsus2

1.

Falling Down - 7 - 1
PGM0313

57

Falling Down - 7 - 5
PGM0313

Falling Down - 7 - 7
PGM0313

REALITY

Elec. Gtrs. 1 & 3 tuned: Elec. Gtr. 2 tuned down 1/2 step:

⑥ = A♭ ③ = D♭   ⑥ = E♭ ③ = G♭
⑤ = E♭ ② = G♭   ⑤ = A♭ ② = B♭
④ = B♭ ① = D♭   ④ = D♭ ① = E♭

Music by MICHAEL MUSHOK,
AARON LEWIS, JOHN APRIL
and JONATHAN WYSOCKI
Lyrics by AARON LEWIS

Moderately ♩ = 106

Intro:

Em (9)

*Music sounds a half step lower than written.

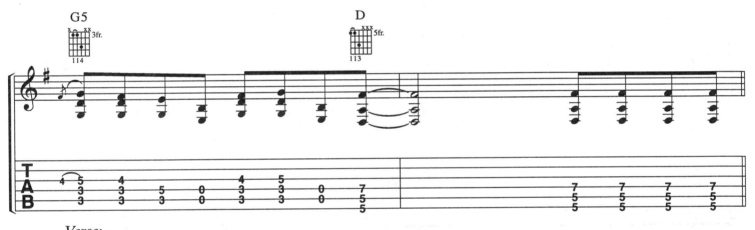

Verse:

w/Rhy. Fig. 1 *(Elec. Gtr. 1) 4 times, simile*

1. The lights are on but you're not home.
2. So you se - date and drown in vain.

62

Reality - 5 - 3
PGM0313

TONIGHT

Elec. Gtrs. 1 & 2 tuned:

⑥ = B♭ ③ = D♭
⑤ = E♭ ② = G♭
④ = A♭ ① = B♭

Elec. Gtr. 3 tuned down 1/2 step:

⑥ = E♭ ③ = G♭
⑤ = A♭ ② = B♭
④ = D♭ ① = E♭

Music by MICHAEL MUSHOK,
AARON LEWIS, JOHN APRIL
and JONATHAN WYSOCKI
Lyrics by AARON LEWIS

Moderately fast ♩ = 126
Intro:

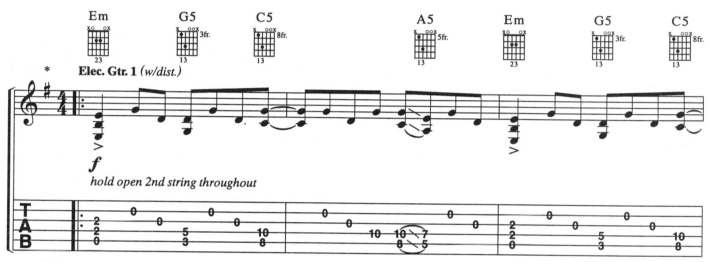

*Music sounds a half step lower than written.

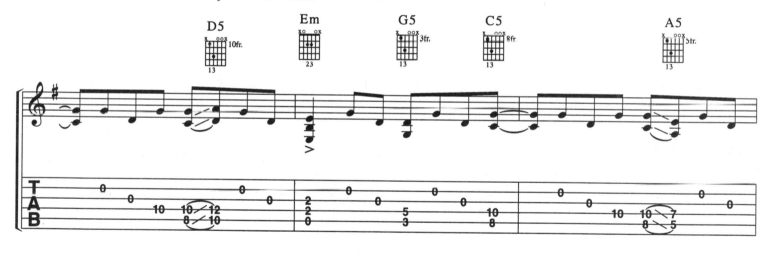

66

68

Tonight - 7 - 4
PGM0313

COULD IT BE

Music by MICHAEL MUSHOK,
AARON LEWIS, JOHN APRIL
and JONATHAN WYSOCKI
Lyrics by AARON LEWIS

Elec. Gtrs. 1 & 2 tuned:

⑥ = A♭   ③ = D♭
⑤ = D♭   ② = E♭
④ = A♭   ① = A♭

Elec. Gtr. 3 tuned down 1/2 step:

⑥ = E♭   ③ = G♭
⑤ = A♭   ② = B♭
④ = D♭   ① = E♭

Moderately ♩ = 104

Intro:

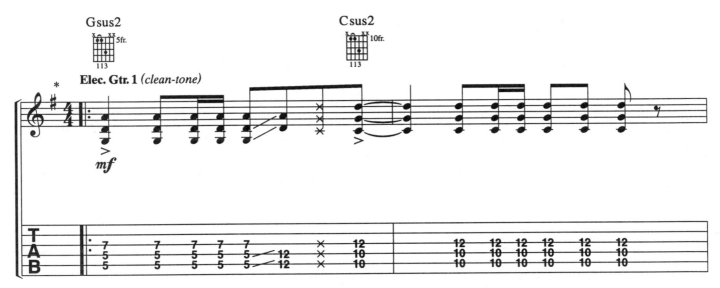

*Music sounds a half step lower than written.

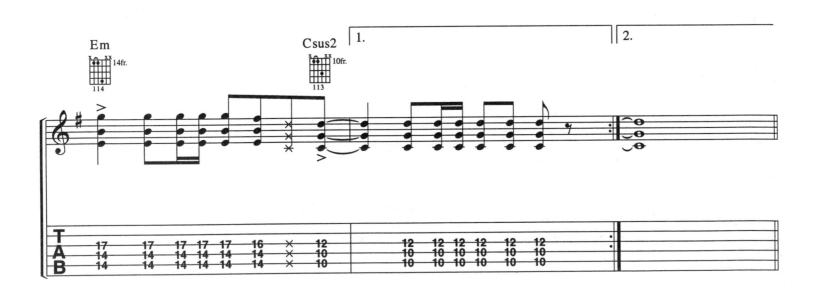

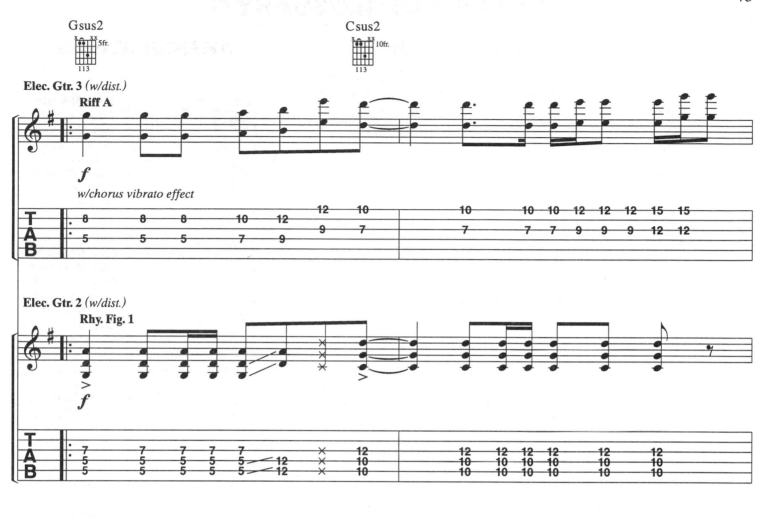

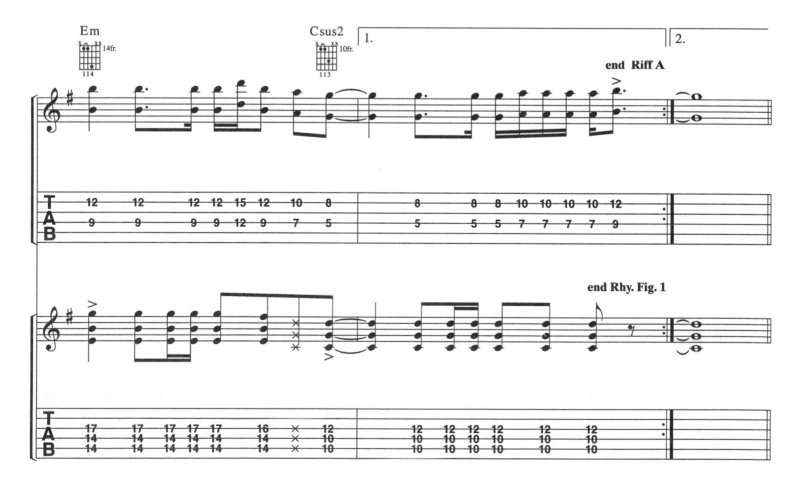

74

Could It Be - 6 - 4
PGM0313

76

Could It Be - 6 - 5
PGM0313

w/Rhy. Fig. 3 *(Elec. Gtr. 2) simile*
w/Riff C *(Elec. Gtr. 3) simile*

gain. I just can't get them__ through__ my head.___
gin to do the things that__ I____ have said.___

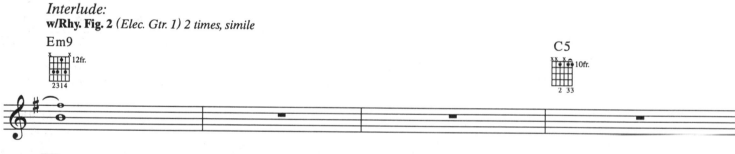

___ There's just too man - y voic - es. ___ I'm__ sor - ry.___
___ And for this____ ___

Interlude:
w/Rhy. Fig. 2 *(Elec. Gtr. 1) 2 times, simile*

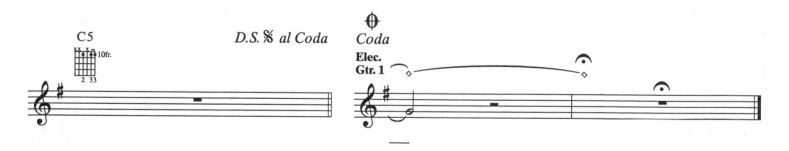

So, there's some truth to__ what__ you_____ say.___

D.S. % al Coda   *Coda*

Could It Be - 6 - 6
PGM0313

BLOW AWAY

Music by MICHAEL MUSHOK,
AARON LEWIS, JOHN APRIL
and JONATHAN WYSOCKI
Lyrics by AARON LEWIS

All gtrs. tuned:

⑥ = A♭   ③ = D♭
⑤ = E♭   ② = G♭
④ = B♭   ① = B♭

Moderately ♩ = 94

Intro:

N.C.

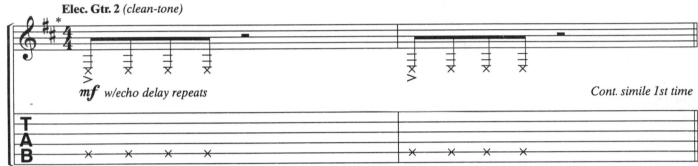

*Music sound a half step lower than written.

*Implied harmony.

Verse3:
So now the walls are closing in
Because in life you sink or swim.
Sometimes these shoes
Don't feel right in my head.
Feel like a book that can't be,
A book that can't be,
A book that can't be read.
(To Chorus:)

INTRO

All gtrs. tuned:

⑥ = A♭ ③ = D♭
⑤ = D♭ ② = E♭
④ = A♭ ① = A♭

Music by MICHAEL MUSHOK,
AARON LEWIS, JOHN APRIL
and JONATHAN WYSOCKI
Lyrics by AARON LEWIS

*Music sounds a half step lower than written.

Intro - 5 - 1
PGM0313

1.2.

3.

Verse:
w/Rhy. Fig. 1 *(Elec. Gtr. 1) 2 times, simile*
D

end Rhy. Fig. 1

1. Thank you to____ the peo - ple in____ my life____
2. F*** you to the jad - ed and fake.____

Cont. simile

B♭5

____ for put - ting up____ with me.____
____ Like to see what you____ would do.____

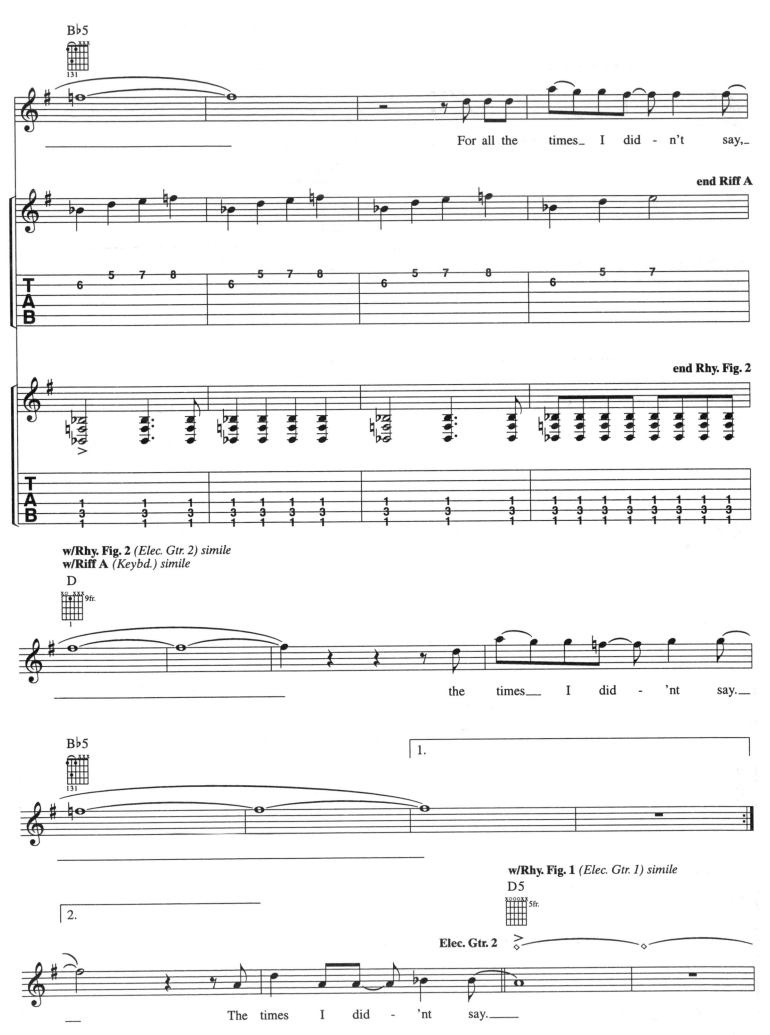

For all the times_ I did - n't say,_

end Riff A

end Rhy. Fig. 2

w/Rhy. Fig. 2 *(Elec. Gtr. 2) simile*
w/Riff A *(Keybd.) simile*

the times_ I did - 'nt say._

1.

w/Rhy. Fig. 1 *(Elec. Gtr. 1) simile*

2.

Elec. Gtr. 2

The times I did - 'nt say.___

GUITAR TAB GLOSSARY **

TABLATURE EXPLANATION

READING TABLATURE: Tablature illustrates the six strings of the guitar. Notes and chords are indicated by the placement of fret numbers on a given string(s).

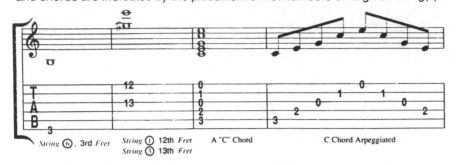

String ⑥ , 3rd Fret

String ① 12th Fret
String ③ 13th Fret

A "C" Chord

C Chord Arpeggiated

BENDING NOTES

HALF STEP: Play the note and bend string one half step.*

PREBEND AND RELEASE: Bend the string, play it, then release to the original note.

WHOLE STEP: Play the note and bend string one whole step.

RHYTHM SLASHES

STRUM INDICA-TIONS: Strum with indicated rhythm.

The chord voicings are found on the first page of the transcription underneath the song title.

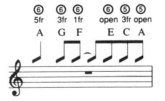

INDICATING SINGLE NOTES USING RHYTHM SLASHES: Very often single notes are incorporated into a rhythm part. The note name is indicated above the rhythm slash with a fret number and a string indication.

*A half step is the smallest interval in Western music; it is equal to one fret. A whole step equals two frets.

**By Kenn Chipkin and Aaron Stang

ARTICULATIONS

HAMMER ON: Play lower note, then "hammer on" to higher note with another finger. Only the first note is attacked.

PULL OFF: Play higher note, then "pull off" to lower note with another finger. Only the first note is attacked.

LEGATO SLIDE: Play note and slide to the following note. (Only first note is attacked).

PALM MUTE: The note or notes are muted by the palm of the pick hand by lightly touching the string(s) near the bridge.

ACCENT: Notes or chords are to be played with added emphasis.

DOWN STROKES AND UPSTROKES: Notes or chords are to be played with either a downstroke (⊓) or upstroke (∨) of the pick.